I am delighted that Tokunbo Emmanuel has developed this thought-provoking series. I am always blessed with the clarity of his writing and the power of his insights. *The Wells of Isaac* will not disappoint.

Dr. Hugh Osgood
Churches in Communities (United Kingdom)

God has given Tokunbo Emmanuel a timely message for the Church today. Anyone who digests the truths in *The Well-digger Trilogy* will experience a paradigm shift towards purposeful Christian living.

Bishop Abraham Olaleye
Elijah Commission (Nigeria)

Tokunbo Emmanuel has helped us to find reproducible principles and patterns in the life of Isaac. He has shown us how we can function and flourish in famine by following specific divine instructions. Just as Isaac obeyed God, sowed his seed, and was persistent in digging wells until he regained the territory he was destined to possess, you too can arrive at your 'Rehoboth' in God by applying the principles in this book.

Gideon Mba
Manifold International Church (Nigeria)

We all must, sooner or later, go through the extremities of life. At such times, only our relationship with God and the truths we have learnt from Him will see us through. *The Wells of Isaac* is a timely work that will help us, individually and corporately, to be consistent in purpose and passion, tenacious in the face of life's circumstances, faithful in and out of season, and constant whether we are full or hungry. Please treat this book as an antidote to the present laxity that seems to suffocate life from our divine encounters with the Holy Spirit.

Ola-Kris Akinola
Bethel Community Church (South Africa)

THE **WELLS** OF
ISAAC

Tokunbo Emmanuel

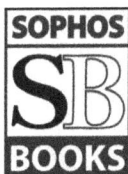

SOPHOS
SB
BOOKS

Raising the voice of Wisdom!

The Wells of Isaac
Copyright © 2012 by Tokunbo Emmanuel
Revised 2017

Published by
SOPHOS Books
163 Warbank Crescent
Croydon
United Kingdom
CR0 0AZ

All Scripture quotations are taken from the *New King James Version* of the Bible. Copyright © 1982 by Thomas Nelson. Used by permission.

Scriptures marked NASB are taken from the *New American Standard Bible*. Copyright © 1960 by The Lockman Foundation. Used by permission.

All rights reserved. No part of this publication may be reproduced, stored in a retrieval system, or transmitted in any form or by any means, mechanical, electronic, photocopying or otherwise without the prior written consent of the copyright owner.

ISBN 978-1-905669-84-4

Cover design by *Maestro Creativity*
Printed in the EU

CONTENTS

To Linda,

Destiny,

Daniel &

David

my well-digging partners.

AUTHOR'S PREFACE

This book is the second title in the *Well-digger Trilogy* that started with *The Secret of Abraham* in 2006. Although it is the second in line, it came after *The Greatest Well-digger in the World,* which was first released in 2007. I am grateful to God for this message of significance that He has committed to me for my generation. These Well-digger books capture its essence.

Please note that *The Wells of Isaac,* in the manner of the other titles, has been written as a *spiritual concentrate*; meaning that it will require deliberate and active times of meditation for proper assimilation and relevant application. It is not meant for casual reading neither will it serve the purpose of revelation knowledge alone. The mission of this book is to transform the mind and provoke a pursuit of purpose for the glory of God. To whichever degree the Holy Spirit accomplishes these in the lives of readers, my joy will know no bounds.

I am grateful to family, friends, mentors, colleagues and readers of my writings—too many names to mention—everyone who, over the years, has consistently encouraged and supported me as I focused my efforts on completing the digging of a *publishing well* in the "land" of my calling. May the Lord continue to remember you for good and grant you the Grace to own many wells in your promised lands.

Finally, I am grateful to my darling wife, Linda, and our dear children, Destiny, Daniel and David; for continuing to persevere with the vision that has taken us away from our comfort zone and is bringing us closer to our *Rehoboth*. I'm loving you everyday!

- Tokunbo Emmanuel

INTRODUCTION

We have more to read in Scripture about Isaac's father, Abraham, than we do of Isaac. We also have more records about his son, Jacob. Nevertheless, one of God's eternal designations is that He is *"the God of Abraham, the God of Isaac, and the God of Jacob;"* this is God's name forever, and His memorial to all generations (Exodus 3:15). God has, therefore, placed the three patriarchs of faith on the same pedestal by naming Himself after all of them.

Isaac played a vital role in the realisation of God's covenant to Abraham. He was a vital link that connected the legacies of the *passing generation* to the destiny of the *coming generation*. Had he not learnt adequately from his father and demonstrated his knowledge before his sons, the lineage of faith would have struggled to remain intact through the transitory years and in the face of constant antagonism. Thank God Isaac was not found wanting in his ability to *learn*, *live* and *leave as a legacy* the knowledge of God's ways.

In our day, we are in dire need of a people after the order of Isaac, a people that will restore the authenticity of The Faith practised by the fathers for the sake of their unborn children. And if the fulfilment of this *restoration agenda* is all history will record about them, it is enough to grant them a place among the great – alongside Abraham, Isaac, Jacob and many others like them.

For this purpose, we need to study Isaac. There is much insight to be gained from the little written about him. The way in which he submitted to his father on the mountain of sacrifice, for instance, laid a divine standard in complete obedience. As a lamb led to the slaughter, he demonstrated how we are to obey our heavenly Father in *all things*. Jesus, our Christ, walked the same path of submission, and in doing so confirmed that Isaac's total surrender is more than a singular, isolated case in Scripture. If we are truly going to be "living sacrifices" before God, we need to emulate Isaac, Jesus and all the heroes of faith who, down the ages, have not treasured their lives above His eternal demands.

Now, apart from the record of how Isaac blessed his sons, Jacob and Esau, *"concerning things to come"* (a feat done "by faith" according to Hebrews 11:20; see also Genesis 27), there is one other main detail about his sojourn from which we can learn wisdom. Scripture devoted a whole chapter to this snapshot from Isaac's life and it is this chapter, Genesis 26, that we seek to explore in this book.

This single chapter unveils many attributes about Isaac, as well as his role in preserving the covenant lineage. For those who have read *The Secret of Abraham*, it is apparent that Isaac learnt from his father what he needed to do to possess the land of promise. He understood the covenant that God made with him and devoted his life to walking in and realising it. As I wrote in the first treatise, *the secret of Abraham [is] revealed in the life of his son.* It is now time to explore this solitary life and learn more about the secret by which Abraham lived and possessed the promised land.

Today, we can say that, of a truth, Abraham was a well-digger; Isaac was a well-digger and Jacob, the third generation from Abraham, was also a well-digger. Hundreds of years after Jacob, communities still benefited from one of the wells that he dug in his lifetime (John 4:11,12). Isaac upheld this generational testimony with his life and blood.

So, here is Isaac before us, the quiet patriarch whose short story speaks volumes about purpose, strength and determination. Anyone who desires to possess their land of promise and become a transformer of regions must learn to imitate him. You can be sure that the principles that were functional in Isaac's life were the same principles taught by God and applied by Abraham and Jacob.

It's now over to you!

Join the Isaac Generation!

At the end of each chapter, we will, by way of application and summary, invite you to join the *Isaac Generation*. This is simply a call for you to identify with the truth and principles by which he lived, and aim for a status of significance as he did.

Holy Spirit, through the inspired writings of David, invited us to join, as it were, the Generation of Jacob; *"the generation of those who seek Him, who seek Your face"* (Psalm 24:6). In other words, we are encouraged to emulate the quest of Jacob and seek God's *presence* rather than His *presents*.

Again, through the writings of Paul, the Spirit testified that *"those who are of faith are [the generation] of Abraham"* (Galatians 3:7 *author's application*). Adding a third witness, God's word encourages us expressly to *"imitate those who through faith and patience inherit the promises"* (Hebrews 6:12).

There is much to discover from the life of Isaac and his type needs to increase upon the earth. So, *The Wells of Isaac* is a clarion call *by* and a divine invitation *from* God's Holy Spirit:

Come and identify with the faith of Isaac and be prepared to emulate his well-digging exploits.

As you meditate on these words, may you hear the Spirit calling you, and respond with all your heart.

1

SUSTAINED IN FAMINE

(Genesis 26:1-10)

That which people are made of becomes evident during the extremities of life. At one end, there are seasons of insufficiency, and on the other, times of abundance. The uninformed are quick to desire the latter over the former, but wisdom teaches that both can destroy if the inner life of a man is not anchored to God.

A wise man once asked for neither riches nor poverty, but for that which is sufficient for life. These were his reasons: *"Lest I be full and deny You, and I say, Who is the Lord? Or lest I be poor and steal, and profane the name of my God"* (Proverbs 30:8,9).

Another wise man said, *"I know how to be abased, and I know how to abound. Everywhere and in all things I have learned both to be full and to be hungry, both to abound and to suffer need"* (Philippians 4:12). The extremes that one abhorred, the other mastered.

Our longing, therefore, should not be for the abundance of this life just because we judge that prosperity is better than poverty; neither should it be for poverty because we are of the mind that it is a sign of spirituality; our longing should be for and intimate relationship with God, who is our true sustenance in times of famine as well as times of plenty. In Him we can be content and victorious no matter the state we find ourselves.

The life of Isaac demonstrates this truth because he experienced, as it were, both ends of the economic spectrum. In this chapter, we will learn how he responded to one extreme (famine), and in the next we will consider the other (abundance).

Famines are unfavourable circumstances that threaten the existence of man. When the heavens give little or no rain, the land becomes barren and the earth withholds its fruit. At other times, food and water shortages, a major feature during famines, are induced during times of conflict and sieges. Without water or food, man's survival is a hopeless affair.

The natural reaction of the *natural* man in such austere conditions is to gravitate towards the scent of water and the aroma of food—shifts that are dictated by the five senses. It is common-sense to the natural man to flee a famine-infested land for a land of perceived abundance.

However, ever since Abraham, Isaac's father, responded to the call of God, his walk was no longer a *natural* walk. The faith that Isaac inherited did not depend on the function of his senses. This faith rested on a deeper "sense," one that was tuned to and responds to the voice of God. It was crucial that Isaac heard from God before making a decision dictated by his feelings.

Decisions are make-or-break moments, especially those that impact the course of life. They can either establish your steps on the pathway of purpose or cause time-wasting detours away from the land of promise. *It is not wise to live by natural instinct when you have access to supernatural direction.* Some detours have consequences that are costlier than others, but why wait to find out the outcome of your choice when you can lean on the One who knows the end from the beginning?

Abraham, in his day, faced the same famine test and his reaction was one of the mistakes he made in life. He did not wait for God's voice to lead him, but went *down* to Egypt in search of greener pastures (Genesis 12:10). Even though he increased in material possessions during his sojourn in Egypt, one of the slave girls his wife acquired later became a snare that nearly hijacked the purpose of God for his life. Till today, we are still reeling from the effects of Abraham's rash decision during famine.

It was now Isaac's turn to face the *same* famine test. It is not unusual for children to encounter the same challenges that their parents could not overcome. Fathers should, in this light, be motivated to fight and win today so their children would not need to fight tomorrow. Because Abraham did not do too well during his famine test, Isaac had to face it in his time. Also, because Abraham "failed" the test of compromise when he claimed Sarah was his sister, Isaac had to face it in Gerar too (Genesis 26:6-11).

We will all face the famine test at one point or the other in our lives, times when circumstances are unfavourable. No one is immune to these temporary, external conditions. Sometimes, it is the enemy of our purpose who orchestrates these occurrences with the sole aim of taking us out of the remit of our calling. Nonetheless, whether they are natural, self-induced or demonic in nature, the essence of the famine test is to prove whether we trust in the Lord who is able to sustain in famine.

Indeed, God can prevent famines altogether, or with a word of His command, change dryness into abundance in an instant. But He will rather sustain us *in* famine and lead us by His voice *through* it into blessings that abide. Those who learn to overcome unbearable circumstances in times of famine are better equipped to stand in times of plenty. Impulsively avoiding famines by every means is a sign of weakness and not the strength of wisdom.

Notice that Isaac's *initial reaction* to the famine was through his senses. He moved to Gerar. This land of the Philistines, while in the boundary of his promised land, was also affected by the famine. As the pressures of survival tightened around Isaac, it was not long before he began to entertain the thought of going all the way to luscious Egypt.

It was at this point that God spoke. *Oh that God will speak whenever we are at the verge of deviating from the path of purpose!* Evidently, Isaac, knowing his father's story, had struggled with what seemed the natural thing to do – go down to *Egypt* – hence the reason why he first moved to *Gerar*. But when conditions did not improve in Gerar, he resigned himself to surviving in Egypt. God saw his heart, and intervened with clear instructions. What would have happened if, like Abraham, Egypt was Isaac's first destination and not Gerar?

The prophet Isaiah has spoken God's eternal opinion on this matter:

"*Woe to the rebellious children, says the Lord...*

who walk to go down to Egypt,
and have not asked my advice."

(Isaiah 30:1,2)

"Woe to those who go down to Egypt for help...
but who do not look to the Holy One of Israel, nor
seek the Lord!...
Both he who helps will fall, and he who is helped
will fall down; they all will perish together."

(Isaiah 31:1-3)

The tensions of faith are always highest in times of famine because the line that divides absolute trust in God from reliance on human understanding is thin. It is good practice, therefore, to put God first "in all your ways." Give Him first priority in moments of decision. Why consult Him *after* you have made up your mind about what to do and where to go? God will never lead astray; He knows how to direct your paths through the wilderness and into the Promised Land.

God will always guide the sincere in heart. Isaac did not hide the struggles he was having about deciding where to find pasture. Egypt was the logical destination, but Isaac wanted to remain in the boundaries of God's will, hence Gerar. Just like the blind man in Jesus' day, who believed but needed help for his unbelief, Isaac's honesty paved the way for God's direction.

This reveals the beauty of praying from the heart. There is no point in hiding doubt and fear from God when they reside in the secret places of the mind. He sees them anyway, so why not be open to God and receive His help? God helped Isaac with a timely word. He is ever-faithful even when we are faithless.

This point cannot be overstated. The advantage Isaac had over any other person facing the same dry circumstances was that he was in covenant with God. He was not facing his hardship all by himself. Such is the nature of covenants; that either in times of plenty or seasons of insufficiency, the two covenant parties remain committed to each other. God never leaves us in adversity. Instead, it is at such times that He manifests His awesome power to save.

"The Lord knows the days of the upright, And their inheritance shall be forever. They shall not be ashamed in the evil time, And in the days of famine they shall be satisfied. "

(Psalm 37:18,19)

The question is: *How is God's power made manifest in times of famine?* Simply, God's sustaining power is released through the words that He speaks. Thankfully, Isaac was in the place where he could receive God's word of instruction. It does not matter the severity of the famine; what matters is what God is saying *in* and *during* the famine. This is the secret of sustenance and turnaround.

God does not speak to us when we go "down" to Egypt. Better put, when we pitch our tents in far away Egypt, we will find it difficult to hear God when He speaks. The few that heard God in the boundaries of Egypt, people like Moses and Joseph the surrogate father of Jesus, are those who were specifically led *to* Egypt for a season. *Oh that our hearts will cease to wonder away from the place where God speaks!* Surely, the best place to dwell is the secret place of the Most High, under the shadows of the Almighty. In this place, the heart will *always* hear His voice.

This, then, is how God sustains in famine; this is the first secret among secrets: *He guides His own from the inner wellspring of the covenant and the riches of His presence.* Out of these will flow wisdom, vision and strategy that will lead to abundance and ultimately turn the famine into a pool of blessing. If a child of covenant will prize above all things the Lord who dwells and speaks from *within*, even when circumstances are unbearable *without*, not only will he or she be kept alive in famine, the unfavourable will in time give way to the favourable through the application of divine wisdom for divine exploits.

Famines can never overcome the person who is sustained from within. If your sustenance comes from your circumstances, surely a famine could kill. But the well of God's presence never runs dry; from this inner well, Isaac thrived when everything else around him dried up.

This is where true blessedness starts – the wellspring of life that flows from the secret place of the heart. From here Isaac was sustained until his circumstances changed.

God's instructions are the key to life. They connect the obedient to His wisdom, power and provision. Those who disregard instruction set themselves up for destruction that is sometimes irreversible. God's instructions are also specific. "Stay *here*. Do not go *there*." Specific instruction, therefore, requires specific obedience.

The interrelationship between instruction and obedience is a spiritual dynamic that keeps the covenant of God alive in the life of the believer. It is the sure sign of a divine partnership that can never be defeated no matter the severity of the famine.

Waiting on God for instruction is not a sign of weakness. Rather it is an evidence of faith in the divine presence. For sure, Isaac could have, with sheer effort, made a way for himself in Egypt, but what is the point of succeeding outside the covenant? Moreover, why exert strength and expend resources in a place that is void of God's *Blessing*? The Blessing of God is located nowhere else than the place where His instructions lead.

There is, therefore, a place called *there*; the specific place where the voice of God pinpoints. In this place, the favour and provision of God is to be found. In this place, the *efforts* of man are blessed by the *pronouncements* of

God. In times of famine, you need to be in the place called *there*.

When the Lord appeared to Isaac, He said emphatically, *"Do not go down to Egypt; live in the land of which I shall tell you. Dwell in this land, and I will be with you and bless you…"* (Genesis 26:2,3). God's presence and Blessing are in the place He pinpoints.

During a famine in Elijah's days, God said to His prophet, *"Get away from here and turn eastward, and hide by the Brook Cherith, which flows into the Jordan. And it will be that you shall drink from the brook, and I have commanded the ravens to feed you* **there***"* (1 Kings 17:3,4). This commanded Blessing was directed to a specific place, and Elijah had to be in the place to receive it. When, after a while, the brook dried up, *"the word of the Lord came to him saying, Arise, go to Zarephath, which belongs to Sidon, and dwell* **there***. See, I have commanded a widow* **there** *to provide for you"* (1 Kings 17:8,9). Again, the provision of God is in the place called *there!*

The safest place to be, especially in times of famine, is in the will of God; the place where His voice leads. In this place, destiny is secure.

In this place, the covenant is affirmed. In any other place, there are no guarantees.

A Hebrew man called Elimelech followed his survival instincts and left Bethlehem because of famine. He and his family went to dwell in the country of Moab. He left the covenant land for the accursed land, not by *instruction* but by *compulsion*. He was pressured by negative circumstances and he yielded to their directives. Sadly, he and his two sons died in Moab. The presence of God was not with them to sustain (Ruth 1:1-5). *The safest place to be is in the will of God.*

You may never be sure how God will make provision when you obey Him, but you can be sure that He will. He can send ravens to feed you, rain down fresh bread from heaven, command water to flow from a rock or speak to the land to yield its abundance. It does not matter *how* He chooses to sustain us in famine; we only need to be sure that He is able to do so.

Famines are never forever. They are only around for a season. However how long the season lasts, the one who abides in God's presence and obeys His instructions will out-

last the length of the famine. The abundance
that sustains him from within will sooner or
later break out and transform the very land in
which he dwells.

Join the Isaac Generation!

Heaven is desperate for a people who are persuaded that neither poverty nor prosperity can separate them from the love of God; a people who seek God's mind at all times and only do what He instructs them to do. They are not moved by sight but by faith in the word of God. They have the well of God's presence in their heart and from this secret place they are adequately sustained. This is the *Isaac Generation* and you can be a part.

How do you react when times are hard?

Do you wait on God to lead you when you get to the crossroads of life?

Are you confident that God can sustain you in times of famine?

*Where is the place called **there** for you, the place where God is trying to position you for unlimited provision?*

2

EMPOWERED FOR INCREASE

(Genesis 26:12-14)

God rules over *all* situations. He created all things visible out of things that had not yet appeared. Before the created things came to be, they were inside Him; when He spoke them forth, they became. Anyone in covenant with God will experience this dimension of His divine working; such a person will rule over his circumstances, no matter how severe.

Out of the unseen well of the heart, Isaac was sustained in famine. He made God his abode and resisted the temptation to chart his own course. He chose to obey God and stayed in the place he was instructed to stay. In response to his obedience, God spoke; and the word released changed Isaac's circumstances forever. In the same way, God will speak to anyone who belongs to Him.

> *"Dwell in this land, and I will be with you and bless you… So Isaac dwelt in Gerar."*

(Genesis 26:3)

When a person locates the place where God's instructions are directing him, and in obedience stays there, two things occur: the *presence* and the *Blessing* of God abide with him. The presence of God will always be found in the place of obedience, and the Blessing of God will always manifest in the place of His presence. It is difficult to access the Blessing when in disobedience.

Disobedience attracts a curse; obedience attracts the Blessing. When the manifest presence of God is absent, curses find a resting place; when the manifest presence of God is present, *blessings* find a resting place. An abiding curse will ultimately lead to death if not reversed; the abiding Blessing will ultimately lead to life that cannot end.

Understand, therefore, what God said to Israel, Isaac's descendants:

"Behold, I set before you today a blessing and a curse: the blessing, if you obey the commandments of the Lord your God which I command you today; and the curse, if you do not obey the commandments of the Lord your God, but turn aside from the way which I command you today..."

(Deuteronomy 11:26-28)

Again He said to them through Moses,

"I call heaven and earth as witnesses today against you, that I have set before you life and death, blessing and cursing; therefore choose life, that both you and your descendants may life."

(Deuteronomy 30:19)

You have the power to choose where your life will end – in life or in death. When you make the right choice, you will have the right end. Famines are not an excuse for wrong choices. External pressure need not determine your internal decisions. External pressure is only for a moment; internal decisions have a much longer lifespan. It is foolish to forfeit eternal blessings because of temporal hardship.

Evidently, Isaac chose life and blessings; he obeyed God and "dwelt in Gerar." The presence of God was with him because he obeyed, and the Blessing of God was with him because of the presence of God.

Whoever God blesses, no man can curse. The most severe of famines cannot destroy a man blessed by God.

The Blessing is an antidote to curses and famines. None of these can withstand the power of the Blessing of God.

The Blessing is the creative power of God encapsulated in the word of His mouth. When released upon a man, nothing in this life can stop the man from becoming all that God's Word says he is. Its power is not quantifiable. It is indestructible and unstoppable. It is a thousand times more powerful than the forces than reside in an atom! It is the supernatural power of God that flows from the inner well of the covenant and rests upon the obedient among men.

Oh, the Blessing! It is God's divine presence in a man that empowers him to prosper in this life. Such a man will prosper in spite of famine because he is already prosperous within. He is *empowered to increase*; blessed to be fruitful. And to reiterate, there is no adverse situation that can hinder the working of this creative force. It is only a matter of time: The Blessing will always overcome adversity and crush insufficiency.

This is how God squashed the famine that threatened Isaac and his household: He empowered him to increase in a barren land.

> *"Then Isaac sowed in that land, and reaped in the same year a hundredfold; **and the Lord blessed him**. The man began to prosper, and continued prospering until he became very prosperous."*

> ### *(Genesis 26:12,13)*

Isaac started with *seeds*. By faith he planted them in a dry ground. The presence and Blessing of God rested upon the seeds and he reaped a bountiful harvest.

Many think that the way out of a famine is for God to supernaturally make material provision available in abundance. If God does not rain down quail from heaven or turn the severe famine around overnight, then He is not doing anything. Surely, God can do these, but for the man who is learning the ways of God; for the one who will ultimately possess the land of promise, the operations are different.

The former is desperate for God's *blessings* – miraculous provision that immediately ends the need of the moment – while the latter is working with God's *Blessing* – divine empowerment to produce blessings from seeds and put an end to needs for a lifetime.

Isaac, the blessed man, sowed in a land of famine and he received blessings of a bountiful harvest. *The Blessing* produced *the blessings*. Once again, the Blessing of God empowered him to increase.

It does not matter how little seed a blessed man starts with; the Blessing of God's presence will cause him to increase bountifully. A truly blessed person does not despise the days of little beginnings because little will eventually become much by virtue of the Blessing.

The Blessing will work on wheat as well as business ideas. The wheat seed will produce much wheat, and the idea of a bakery business will produce much bread. Surely, God *"supplies seed to the sower, and bread for food."* As long as one is in the land of one's calling, God will always bless the handiwork of the blessed.

The Blessing will empower you to increase! Irrespective of your circumstances, God will give you seed to sow and make you fruitful in the land.

"The power to make wealth" (Deuteronomy 8:18 NASB), the power to increase, is given by God to those who are willing and obedient. No matter the field; no matter the seed; this divine power will always work.

The increments that the Blessing produce are not linear; that is, they are not measured in only one dimension. The increments of the blessed man are rather exponential; they are multi-dimensional in nature. Any seed blessed by God will not only produce fruit, but the fruit will itself contain seed that is already blessed by God. This is the exponential dimension of God's blessings; *ever-increasing increase!* No famine can withstand the awesome power that is released by the outworking of God's Blessing!

Evidently, the Blessing was at work in the life of Isaac, because *"the man began to prosper, and continued prospering until he became very prosperous"* (Genesis 26:13). He was empowered to increase exponentially and he did not stop increasing.

It does not matter how difficult the circumstance or how few the seeds, the presence and Blessing of God will always make the difference. Of Abraham, Isaac's father, God said, *"I called him alone, and blessed him and **increased him"*** (Isaiah 51:2). And because this increase had no end, it overflowed into Isaac's life; from Isaac's life it overflowed into Jacob's life; from Jacob it continued to increase into *"all the families on earth"* through the Seed, which is the Christ.

Isaac started from a position of lack, but ended up with *"possessions of flocks and possessions of herds and a great number of servants"* (Genesis 26:14). This is the testimony of a man blessed by God! This can be your testimony too.

Join the Isaac Generation!

Heaven is seeking a generation of blessed people; blessed because of the *presence* and *Blessing* of God in their life, the result of their unrestrained obedience to His instructions. These are people who prioritise fellowship with God over the material blessings of God. They seek God's face and not His hands. They are a people who know the gain of godliness with contentment. They do not despise the days of little beginnings because they are empowered to increase and keep on increasing. They sow their seeds by the leading of God and the Blessing of God causes them to prosper against all odds. This is the *Isaac Generation* and you can be a part.

What value are you placing on the manifest presence of God in your life?

What seed do you have in your hands to sow in your season of draught? What idea is God leading you to pursue?

Do you see yourself as Blessed of God or in need of His blessings?

Where do you see yourself in a year's time with God's Blessing on your life?

3

THE LIMITATIONS OF PROSPERITY

(Genesis 26:15-17)

Choosing to obey God's directives will release the pronouncement of God over the life of the obedient. This pronouncement is never made in vain. Any word that *"goes forth from my mouth,"* God has said, *"shall not return to me void, but it shall accomplish what I please, and it shall prosper in the thing for which I sent it"* (Isaiah 55:11).

So, when God told Isaac *"I will be with you and bless you,"* the power to increase was in that word. It was down to Isaac whether he would receive the word or not. Evidently, he received, believed and acted upon it. The promise mixed with faith inside him and he prospered by reason of the word.

The prosperity Isaac had *inside* him, the covenant-well that resided *within* him, was not affected by the famine *around* him. Instead, his inner prosperity changed his outer reality. He subdued the famine and became a great man of great substance.

It is worth reiterating that Isaac's spiritual prosperity was what produced his material prosperity. The material is always subject to the spiritual, which is why the famine was not much of an issue while it persisted. The famine exerted pressure on Isaac quite alright, but he was anchored to God and was able to withstand it. He had learnt that neither abasement nor abundance was more important than his relationship with God.

When a man understands this truth, he will overcome any kind of famine. His circumstances will not change him; instead he will change his circumstances.

Isaac's material prosperity, therefore, was inevitable because he was already empowered to prosper in his spirit-man. The *"possessions of flocks and possessions of herds and a great number of servants"* were only a by-product of the Blessing of God; they were not the main thing. In fact, they were not a big deal, at least not to the Almighty who blessed him.

Some make material prosperity a major target. They concentrate all their meditation, prayers and earthly pursuits on seeking for things that Gentiles strain for. But Jesus taught His disciples to seek only one thing – the inner life of the kingdom, out of which flows righteousness, power and influence. Anyone who grasps this truth will operate on a level far above his peers. Jesus Himself pursued righteousness and was exalted above all peoples (Hebrews 1:9).

God will always promise us things that transcend our present circumstances. However, without a revelation of the faithfulness of His word, man will lose sight of God's promise and succumb to the pressure that famines exert. Besides, material prosperity will become his loftiest desire. This is the mistake of many who profess faith today.

God promised Abraham much more than

material prosperity. The covenant guaranteed him things that would endure many generations. First, God said to him, *"I will bless you and in you all the families of the earth will be blessed."* As we noted in the previous chapter, this Blessing is more than silver and gold. It is the unseen presence of God that silver and gold cannot buy. It is "the promise of the Spirit" that all who are of the faith of Abraham receive (Galatians 3:14).

There are many things that silver and gold cannot buy; "the promise of the Spirit," the Blessing of Abraham through faith in Christ, is one of them. The Blessing, on the other hand, will produce silver and gold many times over. This is where the limitations of prosperity begin to surface.

In addition to this, the covenant that God made with Abraham promised him *a land* and *a people* that would be His for generations to come. Unequivocally, the Lord had said to him, *"Lift your eyes now and look from the place where you are northward, southward, eastward, and westward; for all the land which you see I give to you and your descendants forever"* (Genesis

13:14,15). Again, material prosperity cannot secure these for any considerable length of time.

Remember that Abraham, at the time of this promise, was a sojourner in the land and was also without child. He was also already *"very rich in livestock, in silver, and in gold"* (Genesis 13:2). However, much more than material prosperity was needed to fulfil the word that God spoke to him. God promised him the land and not just the *produce* of the land. God also promised a covenant people who would occupy the land.

Why get satisfied with *produce* from your land when you have not yet *possessed* the land? Why settle for a house full of purchased servants when you do not yet have a son from your own loins, one after your own kind? It is not enough to acquire possessions *in* the land if you are not ruling *over* the land. These were the perspectives that God established in Abraham. For these reasons God raised him to be a *well-digger*.

Only those who owned wells could lay claim to the land and exercise dominion over it. Even the most prosperous in terms of silver and gold were at the mercy of the land's well-owners.

During their wilderness journeys, when the nation of Israel passed through the territory of Seir, which belonged to the descendants of Esau, God said to them, *"Do not meddle with [Seir], for I will not give you any of their land, no, not so much as one footstep, because I have given Mount Seir to Esau as a possession"* (Deuteronomy 2:5). And since God was not giving them the land, they were not going to dig any wells there. Instead, God instructed them: *"You shall buy food from them with money, that you may eat; and you shall also buy water from them with money, that you may drink"* (Deuteronomy 2:6).

In the land of Seir, Israel could only *purchase* their necessities. Even though they had the money and were very prosperous, the descendants of Esau who *produced* the food and water ruled the land. Consumers are always subject to producers. Water-drinkers are always servants to well-diggers.

Here again is a limitation of prosperity. Those who dig and own wells rule the land

and have direct influence over those who need to survive on the water that they produce. It does not matter how rich water-drinkers are, they will always depend on well-owners.

Well-digging was, therefore, a preoccupation of Abraham. It was the strategic activity that depicted his seriousness in possessing the promise of God. He did not just believe God for the land; he dug wells and became a producer of water in the land. He staked his claim on Canaan and became the pace-setting influence in the communities that formed around his wells.

The reason why God called Abraham and gave him the land by promise was that He wanted a people with distinct values to occupy the region. God did not just promise to multiply Abraham's descendants; He also proved Abraham to ascertain that his descendants after him would imbibe the culture of faith and righteousness that he practiced and lived by.

In other words, the covenant God made with Abraham was not about the prosperity of Abraham; that was just an added benefit. The covenant was more about the mandate to permeate the land with the values of God through the people that will descend from Abraham's loins. This was the basis for and essence of Abraham's calling; this was the reason for the covenant God made with him.

"For I have known him, in order that he may command his children and his household after him, that they keep the way of the Lord, to do righteousness and justice, that the Lord may bring to Abraham what He has spoken to him."

(Genesis 18:19)

Again, prosperity was a mere by-product of the covenant; it was not the reason *for* the covenant; it was never, in itself, the reason. It will never be the motivation from heaven's perspective. The covenant will always produce prosperity, but prosperity cannot produce the covenant. Those who limit their interactions with God to an expectation of earthly blessings do not yet know the heart and purposes of God.

Isaac understood the limitation of prosperity through experience. He discovered that all his wealth meant nothing if he did not own the land and have influence among the people. His silver and gold could not stop the Philistines, who envied him for his wealth, from chasing him out of the land. They could do this because they had stopped all the wells that his father had dug and had claimed ownership of them.

"Now the Philistines had stopped up all the wells which his father's servants had dug in the days of Abraham his father, and they had filled it with earth. And Abimelech said to Isaac, Go away from us, for you are much mightier than we. Then Isaac departed from there and pitched his tent in the Valley of Gerar, and dwelt there."

(Genesis 26:15-17)

Even if Isaac could buy all the water he needed in his lifetime, his achievements would have gone with him into the grave if he did not own some wells in the land; he wouldn't have passed anything substantial unto the coming generation.

Well-diggers are generational-thinkers. They do not just live for themselves; rather, they labour purposefully for those around them and those who will come after them.

Isaac did not allow the riches he had acquired in Gerar to blur his vision of possessing the land and raising a people who feared and worshipped God. He discovered that there is much more to the covenant than surviving famines and making a fortune. These are good, but not good enough.

Believing God for material blessings alone without a vision to possess the land for Him places a limit on how far one can go with God. The Kingdom of God is more than silver and gold; it is more than meat and drink. The Kingdom of God is the permeation of the earth with righteousness, peace, Holy-Spirit-joy and justice. It is the will of God accomplished on earth as it is done in heaven. It is the main thing; prosperity is a mere addition.

Isaac did not seek prosperity; he only sought to obey God. And because he sought to obey God, prosperity sought relentlessly for him and camped abundantly around him. When you seek to possess your land and establish the rule of God among the people in your domain, prosperity will attend to you. When you seek prosperity, it will become a hindrance to a life of purpose, significance and fulfilment.

It is no wonder then that the first thing Isaac did after he was driven from the land into the valley, was to re-open the wells of his father. He began a crusade to reclaim the land that was already promised to him in the covenant. He did not do this just for himself alone, but also, more so, for the generations that would come after him.

Join the Isaac Generation!

Heaven is longing to bring a people into material abundance, but is aware that too many become slaves of abundance. Heaven is seeking a people whose sole desire is the Kingdom of God and its righteousness. Such a people will not only be blessed; they will channel the blessings for the extension of God's dominion on earth. These are a people who understand that their destiny on earth is to rule all things for God's sake and not be ruled by things. They are consumed by a desire to subdue the enemies of God under the feet of Christ. Prosperity will not distract them because they know the purpose of true riches. This is the Isaac Generation and you can be a part.

Are you a slave of money or free from the love of money?

Where is your most desired treasure located, in heaven or on earth?

How do you feel seeing the ungodly controlling different spheres of society?

What vision do you have for the land of your calling?

4

RE-OPENING THE WELLS
OF OLD

(Genesis 26:18)

God is eternal and He works through the generations. He does not just operate in the present, but continues from the past with the future in view. He is the same yesterday, today and forever; and because He remains the same, those who entrust their lives to Him are not subjected to confusion or extinction.

God's purpose also does not change in changing times. He does not change His mind about what He has purposed to achieve, neither does He reduce His standards from one generation to the next. Every generation must rise up to His standards and fulfil their part in the realisation of His eternal purpose.

One of the reasons why God called Abraham and taught him His ways was so that Isaac, the succeeding generation, can learn these ways from Abraham and walk therein. This did not exclude Isaac from learning directly from God; instead it enhanced the things God taught him.

In other words, every godly generation should enable the next to do more for God. There is no need for a generation of people to fight battles that the previous generation have secured the victory for – unless the ground is taken back by the enemy.

If a generation fails to equip the next generation in the purposes of God, or their gains are not adequately preserved, there will be a relapse in the progress that they have made. Such a decline will always threaten to occur when the heroes of a generation finish their work and pass on to glory. Surely, every generation is in a territorial war.

In *The Secret of Abraham*, it was revealed that Abraham possessed the land of Canaan not by mere confession, but by well-digging. He did not dig wells because it was a prestigious thing to do, neither did he engage in well-digging because he needed water for his household. He dug many wells because God had given him the land of Canaan as a possession forever.

Abraham's many wells, together with the favour of God that was on him, established his influence in the land of Canaan – even among a hostile people. Instead of contending against him, his enemies made treaties with him (see Genesis 21:22-34).

God had promised Abraham the land as far as his eyes could see; and being a man of faith and vision, he had dug wells everywhere his feet could take him. He laid solid foundations for the coming generations, first by his *walk* of faith and also by his *work* of well-digging.

However, after his death, the Philistines stopped up all the wells that he had dug, and *"filled them with earth."* They regained much of the territory by reclaiming many of the wells. This further highlights the importance of wells and their significance in land-ownership.

What would have happened if Abraham did

not raise Isaac to understand the covenant and promises of God? Where would Israel be today if Isaac did not grow up with a well-digger mentality? After all, he was rich and well-to-do. He could have survived without concerning himself with the rigours of well-digging. But the covenant of God was more important than personal survival. Isaac needed to confront the problem of stopped wells for the sake of posterity.

Even though the Philistines had blocked all the physical wells that Abraham dug, they had no access to the spiritual well that he had installed in Isaac, his son. Abraham had exemplified a life of sacrifice and worship before his son and his entire household. He had built altars to God and communicated to his family about the covenanted land upon which they sojourned. He raised Isaac in the fear of God, especially when he took him on top of the mountain and offered him to God as a sacrifice. All these became a residue of spiritual life that the Philistine earth could not reach. It was this inner well that sustained Isaac throughout the famine; out of this inner well he enjoyed the peace and guidance of God.

Isaac's spiritual prosperity accomplished for him what his material prosperity could not do. Out of it came an understanding of the importance of possessing the land of Canaan in spite of the Philistines' cruelty. He understood that the Philistines would always have the upper hand if he did not own any wells. He therefore embarked on the task of reopening the wells of his father. He defied the danger in order to preserve the covenant.

Isaac did not just start digging new wells; he first restored the wells dug by his father. He also *"called them by the names which his father had called them."* By this he acknowledged the faith of Abraham, of which he was a benefactor.

Every generation ought to build on the achievements of previous generations. The young should stand on the shoulders of the old and reach higher heights. The offspring of the young should attain greater horizons still. Discontinuity in the outworking of the covenant from one generation to another can ultimately grind the agenda of God to a creeping pace. Instead of life, death will prevail; instead of blessings curses will abound.

Isaac did not remove the ancient landmark of faith that God set for his father. He did not change the standard by which he operated. He also did not seek to possess another land just because the Philistines occupied the land God promised him. No. He chose to contend for the faith of his father and the land of their inheritance. He reopened the wells and restored his rightful ownership of the land.

When God finds a man who is determined not to compromise his stance on the truths he had been taught, He will back such with divine favour. Isaac walked in great favour and had great success in well-digging.

There is a need for every generation to consider whether the faith that they profess is still the same that was delivered unto the fathers of old. Have the tenets of faith shifted? Even subtle distortions will have monumental adverse effects. Isaac did not dig new wells until he reopened the old wells. He made sure that there was continuity in his pursuit of God's covenant and eternal promises.

Join the Isaac Generation!

Heaven is desperate for a people who will earnestly contend for the faith that was once and for all delivered unto the saints; a people passionate about the truths and standards of God. This generation is not satisfied with spiritual stagnation, talk less of spiritual retrogression. They long to advance the Kingdom of God but must first re-establish the purity and simplicity of the gospel of Christ. They are a people of *present truth* that have not put aside *ancient truth*. They cannot tolerate deception, heresies and error; they cannot settle for worldliness and carnality. They consider it a mandate to regain every lost territory and preserve the tenets of faith for coming generations. This is the *Isaac Generation* and you can be a part.

Are you satisfied with popular Christianity that downplays the truths of God?

Are there any spiritual gains from the past that are now in jeopardy?

Are you committed to the purity and simplicity of the gospel of Christ?

Are you opposed to the "old time religion"?

.

5

THE WELL CALLED REHOBOTH

(Genesis 26:19-22)

With the wells of Abraham now open and called by their original names, Isaac was ready to express his *own* well-digger capabilities and possess his *own* territories. Even though he functioned in the same covenant that God had with Abraham and inherited a number of wells from his father, Isaac needed to dig his *own wells* and make his *own contributions* to the establishment of the covenant. He was not satisfied with just maintaining his father's accomplishments; he desired, and rightly so, some achievements that bore his name.

It does not matter how much a generation achieves in possessing the land, every succeeding generation must also seek to possess more territory. Instead of camping around past success, those who live in the present should build upon it. This is how the entire terrain is taken and the word of the Lord fulfilled.

When a generation satisfies itself with past victories, especially when there are still wars to fight, it would soon lose ground to the opposition. The momentum of yesterday can only carry a people to a point if they do not generate momentum of their own.

The inheritance that an accomplished generation stores up for the next is not just the *fruit* of their success, but also the *principles* by which they succeeded. If the children only focus on enjoying yesterday's fruit without applying the principles to produce more fruit, apathy will soon set in and the harvest barn will soon become empty. What a tragedy this could cause for the third or fourth generations! Isaac did not just maintain Abraham's wells; he applied the secret of Abraham and sought to dig more wells.

You were created with a purpose, and the time will surely come for your purpose to seek expression. It does not matter for how long you ignore its existence within, the seeds of purpose that abide in the recess of the heart will eventually long to sprout. There can never be fulfilment in life until these seeds are cultivated into a harvest of achievement.

You were created to be a well-digger and are destined to own some wells. The many wells of your father (if he was not a mere water-drinker) should not deprive you of the joy of digging your own. Why live the life of an insignificant water-drinker when you have it in you to become a well-digger?

Isaac was a *well-digger* who was eager to become a *well-owner*. He wanted to play his part in possessing the land of promise by digging his own wells and calling them by his own names. Nothing was going to deprive him of these well-digging experiences – not the Philistines; not the legacy of his father. He understood the principle and was keen to make use of it. He was also committed to the covenant and was ready to play his own part in establishing it.

The Secret of Abraham teaches that the land God promises a man, the territory to which he has been assigned in life, can only be possessed through well-digging. Until you succeed in digging wells on your land, you cannot claim ownership of it even though it has been promised to you. The transition from a *promised land* to a *possessed land* involves the rigour of well-digging. Those who are not ready to dig wells are also not ready to occupy their land.

God, on His part, will assign the land by promise and through prophecy; man, on his part, must possess the land by faith and through well-digging. Until man possesses the land through well-digging, he cannot exercise lordship over it. Those who own the wells on the land rule the land. Isaac understood the principle and soon set out to dig and name his *first well*.

The moment a man decides to dig his first well in the land of his allotment, opposition will arise to hinder his quest. The enemy of man will rather rule over man than see him rule the land. If he cannot keep man from becoming a hardworking well-digger, he will attempt to frustrate all his efforts and prevent him from owning any well. Isaac met with stiff opposition in his bid to becoming a well-owner.

The enemy's resistance, particularly when you set out to possess your land of promise, is usually a sign that you are moving in the right direction. When nothing is resisting your progress, it is likely you are not making any progress at all.

There is a phase in life, *before* the ownership of the first well, where a state of no-resistance is not a blessing. The experience of zero-resistance could signal stagnation, the acceptance of mediocrity or a rating of insignificance in the eyes of the enemy. If you will excel in the land of your assignment, do not be surprised when you face trials of many kinds. Be prepared to face and overcome everything that will try to hinder you.

Again, you cannot avoid opposition in your land of promise. Some try to avoid opposition by opting for what seems like an easier land to possess. The truth is: *there is no other land for you to possess than the one to which you are assigned by God.* Besides, it is fallacious to think that there are lands that are free from opposition. It is better to *succeed* in your assigned land in spite of opposition than to merely *survive* in an unassigned land and submit to opposition. Well-diggers overcome opposition; water-drinkers are overcome by opposition.

The way Isaac overcame the Philistine opposition was to *focus* on his goal of well ownership and *continue* doing what would help him achieve this goal. He simply continued digging wells. He did not allow himself to be distracted by the Philistines' actions. He ignored them and remained committed to his objectives.

Distraction is a sure killer of purpose. Many times, the enemy will pick a fight with you just to get you off course. When you stop to engage in this kind of battle, you lose time and are drained of energy. So, it is important to discern the good fight and the bad fight of faith. It is a good fight when the Lord is fighting for you, and a bad fight when you are fighting for yourself! When you are tempted to fight for your right and the Lord is showing you a better way, resist the temptation and apply the Lord's wisdom. Temptation, at the end of the day, is a distraction from the path of destiny. Those who discern it for what it is seldom fall into its trap.

Again, it is futile to hope for the absence of battles; and equally pointless to fight in the hope that all enemies will be eradicated. Engaging the Philistines in physical combat in a bid to make them extinct would have been a wrong war to fight at this stage in Isaac's sojourn. Even if Isaac and his household were able to destroy *all* the Philistines, he would have had to deal with another set of enemies – the Hittites or the Amorites, probably. *The face of opposition may change; but the spirit is always the same.*

It is crucial, therefore, to subdue the *spirit of opposition* and place little importance on its face. The moment you succeed in overcoming the spirit of opposition, you will begin to excel in your allotted land and do great exploits for God.

The goal of the spirit of opposition, irrespective of its face, is to snuff out the *well-digger spirit* that you possess. Spirits will always engage spirits. The spirit of opposition wants your spirit to quit in the face of hardship. The spirit of opposition wants your spirit to settle for a life that is far below your potential. The spirit of opposition wants to buffet your spirit to submission. But if, in your spirit, you know who you are, Whose you are and Who is on your side, you will retain your vision of well-ownership and continue digging until your opposition wears itself out.

It did not matter how many times the Philistines contended for the wells of Isaac; the covenant man simply moved on and dug another well. He did not seek for a less stressful land to settle in; he remained in his assigned land and pursued his vision of owning wells and ruling the land.

Isaac's persistence won in the end. He outlasted the opposition and completed the digging of his first well. Those who remain focused on their God-given vision will always prevail over the spirit of opposition. Let the vision of owning your first well in your assigned land inspire you to keep on digging until your adversaries fade to oblivion.

There is a well called your *first well*; the first well in your assigned land that you can call your own; the well that the enemy does not contend for. Truth is, the enemy *cannot* contend for this well because he could not conquer your well-digger spirit.

Everything you ever experienced in the past is preparation for your first well. All the battles, hardship and trials; all of life's lessons and heartfelt sacrifices; every past victory, success and testimony; all of these are leading up to this monumental feat—ownership of your very first well. This is not your father's well but your own, the fruit of *your* vision and hard work.

If the enemy's contentions over your life ever succeed in robbing you of the courage to continue digging; if they manage to make you quit the land altogether, you would never experience the joy of owning and naming your first well. This is the joy of uncontested accomplishment; the breakthrough of a person of purpose.

Your first well, one that is beyond the enemy's disputation, is worth digging for without ceasing. It is the well that establishes you in your allotted land. Can you imagine the sense of fulfilment Isaac had when he realised there were no Philistines in sight to contest for the well?

Isaac had experienced contention at *Esek* and enmity at *Sitnah*, but none of these stopped him from digging yet another well. Realising that the Philistines had now given up the chase, and with much gratitude and satisfaction in his heart, Isaac gave an appropriate name to his first well: *Rehoboth*.

> *And he moved from there and dug another well,*
> *and they did not quarrel over it. So he called its*
> *name Rehoboth, because he said, "For now*
> *the Lord has made room for us, and we shall be*
> *fruitful in the land."*
>
> **(Genesis 26:22)**

Rehoboth means "the Lord has made room" – room for fruitfulness, abundance and self-expression in the land. What an appropriate name for a significant well! Rehoboth was Isaac's testimony; it conveyed his appreciation for God's favour and revealed the full extent of his covenant-driven vision.

Evidently, Isaac's well-digging ambition transcended the need to provide water for his household; he had a vision of possessing the entire land of promise and laying a firm foundation for future generations.

This Rehoboth experience confirmed for Isaac, beyond any iota of doubt, that the promise God made to him and his descendants; the generational vision that set the course of his lineage forever, will surely come to pass. If he could outlast the attacks of the enemy, his offspring will certainly rise above any opposition — as long as they remain true to the values of God.

Rehoboth is every well-diggers dream. It represents the establishment of a life of purpose. It is akin to the table that God prepares for one in the presence of antagonists. It means the platform is set for the well-digger to become all he was created to be. If there are seeds of destiny that are still uncultivated, the time has now come for them to grow and blossom.

Rehoboth is the *beginning* of a fruitful life of purpose, a compensation that makes the sacrifice of obedience and well-digging worthwhile. Although Isaac had endured much opposition, Rehoboth was a worthy compensation. It confirmed him as a man of obedience and faith, a covenant person in his own right after the order of his father.

Rehoboth is a testimony of God's backing.

Rehoboth is the fruit of His presence abiding.

Rehoboth is a declaration of success and victory.

Rehoboth is a celebration of courage and mastery.

Rehoboth is the result of unwavering persistence.

Rehoboth is a statement of tomorrow's intent.

Rehoboth is the beginning of the realisation of purpose.

Rehoboth is a landmark that the enemy cannot oppose.

Whatever else you do, you must dig your first well called Rehoboth.

However long it takes, you must dig your Rehoboth.

Rehoboth is a mark of success that leads to a life of significance. It gives you the necessary leverage to become exceedingly fruitful in your assigned land.

Rehoboth is a manifestation of faith for continuous provision. It is a sure sign of abundant Grace for every good work.

However long it takes, continue digging until you get your own Rehoboth!

Join the Isaac Generation!

Heaven is looking for a people of purpose; a people so consumed with a vision from God that they will not take "no" as an answer from anyone—surely not from themselves. These people are committed to the vision of possessing the land for God. They see their individual assignments as a significant contribution to this heavenly mandate. Therefore, with an unquenchable well-digger spirit, they remain focused and are not easily distracted from their God-given assignments. They understand that God will make room for them if they refuse to quit the race. They outlast the enemy and obtain their Rehoboth. This is the *Isaac Generation* and you can be a part.

Have you finished digging your first well in the land of your calling?

What are the distractions you are facing in your bid to becoming a well-owner?

How are you responding to setbacks in your endeavours to dig your first well?

Can you imagine the joy of acquiring and naming your Rehoboth?

6

LORD OF THE WELLS

Let us appreciate how far Isaac has come in his transformational journey. He started from a situation of need and insufficiency, from a famine that threatened his very existence. Reacting to this trying time, he was close to yielding to the temptation that would have taken him out of his covenant allotment. Egypt beckoned to Isaac, but the intervening voice of God kept him in the land of his calling.

Isaac obeyed the voice of God and began to enjoy divine sustenance through God's Blessing and in spite of the famine. Through faith and obedience, he sowed seeds in a dry and unfavourable ground, and supernaturally moved from insufficiency to enviable abundance in the space of a year.

Isaac did not allow the material prosperity to limit his destiny. He did not satisfy himself with his acquisitions, but realised that contrary to the promise of God to his lineage, the Philistines still controlled the wells in the land.

Isaac understood what this meant; that the Philistines could exert their authority over him (because whoever possessed the wells owned the land). And they did; out of resentment against his prosperity, the Philistines sent Isaac packing from Gerar. Besides, they stopped all the wells dug by his father and reasserted their influence over Canaan territory.

Isaac, fully devoted to the covenant that God made with his father and his descendants, sought to redress the situation and regain the ground that had been lost to the enemy. He embarked on a mission to reopen all the wells of Abraham.

After successfully reopening the wells of Abraham, Isaac became eager to break fresh ground. He had it in him to dig wells of his own and build on the legacy of his predecessor.

Driven by this desire and by the covenant, he stepped out to dig, but his exploits in well-digging once again provoked the envy and fury of the Philistines. They quarrelled with him over the water and took ownership of Sitnah.

Isaac bounced back from this setback and dug another well, but there was contention over this one too. The Philistines, in opposition to Isaac's right to rule the land, claimed Esek was their own. Their brutal aggression, however, did not quench Isaac's well-digger spirit. And since they could not take charge of the courage of his inner man, they could not stop him from digging yet another well.

Without giving in to discouragement or despair, Isaac retained his vision and moved on. He refused to engage in the wrong fight and consequently became an unstoppable well-digger that could not be subdued.

Courageously, he dug yet another well and his enemies backed off for fear. Other men would have succumbed to the pressure of persecution and given up on their covenant position, but not Isaac. So much was at stake. He stood his ground, stirred up his well-digger spirit and dug his Rehoboth.

Isaac was no longer confined by space; he had entered his wealthy place.

Isaac was no longer troubled by opposition; he had outlasted them in the race.

Isaac was no longer lacking in earth's resources; his life was full of heaven's Grace.

From Rehoboth, the place of God's approval, Isaac now had his sight on the entire terrain. He was now a successful well-digger like his father. He had not only *dug* wells, but had also *named* them. Not only did he *dig* and *name* wells, he also *owned* one that was a fruit of *his* vision and efforts.

Isaac dug Rehoboth.

Isaac named Rehoboth.

Isaac owned Rehoboth.

Isaac claimed the land around Rehoboth.

Isaac was no longer a mere sojourner in the land; he had become a *lord of the wells.*

This is what the Philistines dreaded all along. This is what they wanted to prevent. They did not want Isaac to establish his roots in the land and have the opportunity to claim ownership of it. They certainly did not want his influence to spread through the length and breadth of Canaan. But God's hand was with Isaac. With much perseverance, Isaac succeeded in a hostile land. He became lord of Rehoboth and the wells of his father, and thus a lord in the land. He subdued the opposition and stepped into a position of dominion that mere prosperity could not obtain.

"The same night" that Isaac became a lord of the wells, the rightful lord of Rehoboth, God appeared to him and confirmed the covenant between them.

> *"Then he went up from there to Beersheba. And the LORD appeared to him the same night and said, "I am the God of your father Abraham; do not fear, for I am with you. I will bless you and multiply your descendants for My servant Abraham's sake." So he built an altar there and called on the name of the LORD, and he pitched his tent there; and there Isaac's servants dug a well."*

(Genesis 26:23-25)

In this encounter, the Lord was testifying that Isaac had proven himself as a true heir of the Abrahamic covenant. He had walked in the faith of Abraham and applied the secret of dominion. The Lord saw that Isaac was committed to furthering the divine cause for which Abraham was called, which, in essence, was His eternal programme for redeeming the earth and its people; and in turn, the Lord committed Himself to Isaac afresh.

There is a measure of blessing that God commits to everyone on the face of the earth – both the righteous and the unrighteous; there is a greater measure that is meant only for those who are in right standing with Him; there is yet an even greater measure that only those who prove themselves faithful to His cause enjoy. Isaac proved himself faithful just like his father did. He received the affirmation of God's irreversible promise, similar to the one his father received after he was offered to God on the mountain of sacrifice. *Surely, irreversible blessings are reserved only for those who are unreservedly committed to God.*

Isaac's response to God's pronouncement was in the steps of his father. He built an altar to God in that place and *worshipped*. He pitched his tent there for *fellowship* with his household. He also dug *another well* there as an extension of his dominion in the land (Genesis 26:25).

These three activities are the habits and characteristics of a person with a divine mandate: worship, fellowship and well-ownership.

These are also the means by which man was intended to rule the earth for God. None of them are negligible. You cannot embrace one and ignore the rest. It is not enough, for instance, to worship God and not manifest His character in the context of fellowship. Neither is it enough to do these two and not extend His dominion in the earth through well-ownership. Also, if you are digging wells but are uncommitted to the worship of God, what kind of values will your influence promote? *Selah.*

The God-given mandate of man to be fruitful, multiply and have dominion over the earth requires these significant activities. With them, man is destined to become a *lord of the wells* no matter his land allocation. Whatever "land" you are called to possess for God, you can rise and rule through the covenant practices of worship, fellowship and well-ownership.

A lord of the wells is a person of influence. Evidently, Isaac had become a man of influence. So great was his authority in the land that his enemies sought allegiance with him. Surely, *"when a man's ways please the Lord, he makes even his enemies to be at peace with him"* (Proverbs 16:7).

> *Then Abimelech came to him from Gerar with Ahuzzath, one of his friends, and Phichol the commander of his army. And Isaac said to them, "Why have you come to me, since you hate me and have sent me away from you?"*
>
> *But they said, "We have certainly seen that the LORD is with you. So we said, 'Let there now be an oath between us, between you and us; and let us make a covenant with you, that you will do us no harm, since we have not touched you, and since we have done nothing to you but good and have sent you away in peace. You are now the blessed of the LORD.'"*
>
> *So he made them a feast, and they ate and drank. Then they arose early in the morning and swore an oath with one another; and Isaac sent them away, and they departed from him in peace."*

(Genesis 26:26-31)

At one time, Isaac was driven from the land by the Philistines; not too long afterwards, he was recognised as *"the blessed of the Lord."* What had changed? What did Abimelech and his people see in Isaac that made them change their attitude towards him?

Obviously, they saw a man whose spirit could not be defeated by famine, persecution, lack and even prosperity. They saw a man of faith, vision and wisdom. They saw a man who refused to quit or compromise no matter what they did to stop him. They realised that his prosperity was genuine and unquestionable, and his right to the land could no longer be contested.

Perhaps the Philistines also realised that since Isaac left Gerar, their land was no longer favoured as before; that the famine was causing much devastation compared to when Isaac was within their borders. They had no choice but to conclude that the hand of God was upon him.

A man who carries the Blessing of God will be an indispensible blessing to his community. His presence alone, indeed the presence of God in his life, will have a blessed effect on his surroundings. When there is no blessed man in a place, both the people and the land will struggle and suffer. The promise of God to

86   *The Wells of Isaac*

Abraham was *"I will bless you… and you shall be a blessing"* (Genesis 12:2).

Everyone who inherited the Blessing of Abraham walked in this dimension of blessedness; Jacob did, Joseph did, David did, Jesus did, Isaac certainly did... You can also. The people of Gerar knew the difference between Isaac's presence with them and his absence from them.

When a man becomes a lord of the wells in the land of his calling, his standing in society will not be hidden. Even his enemies will notice his good works and acknowledge the goodness of God in his life. They will want to associate with him and benefit from the Grace of God upon him.

Providing a well for the benefit of others is a good work that cannot go unnoticed. Those who benefit from it will endlessly glorify God for the resource and the well-digger's selfless service.

Abimelech came to Isaac with key people in his administration and entered into a treaty with him. Indeed, representatives from the government of nations will seek the favour of a lord of the wells. They will come to learn how to solve the problem of "broken walls" and "desolate communities." Out of the well of a heart soaked in God's presence will flow divine answers to all their enquiries.

Isaac knew the tenets of the covenant God made with his father; that the territory he will possess extended as far as his eyes could see, including *"northward, southward, eastward and westward"* (Genesis 13:14,15). Having now established himself as a well-digger-owner who had heaven's divine help, he continued to dig more wells and extend the territory of his domain. He did not stop at Rehoboth; he moved into other regions in the perimeter of his allotment.

The very day Abimelech and his officials left for Gerar, Isaac, through the efforts of his servants, increased the scope of his dominion by yet another well.

"It came to pass the same day that Isaac's servants came and told him about the well which they had dug, and said to him, "We have found water." So he called it Shebah. Therefore the name of the city is Beersheba to this day"

(Genesis 26:32,33)

Isaac decided not to lose the momentum he had gained in Rehoboth; he decided to press on with his well-digging, land-taking mission. He fortified the foundations upon which future generations would be founded into communities of God-lovers and God-worshipers.

Isaac continued to possess the land of promise through well-digging, and the wells he dug became communities that have remained "to this day."

What a legacy! What impact!

Beersheba, literally, "The Well of the Oath or Well of the Seven," became an important designation in Bible time Israel. It marked the southern border of Israelite territory, while the region of Dan marked the northern border. The phrase *"from Dan even to Beersheba"* later became a reference to the entire land of Israel (see Judges 20:1; 1 Samuel 3:20; 2 Samuel 3:10 etc.).

Today, Beersheba is "the largest city in the Negev desert of southern Israel [and] the seventh-largest city in Israel." Its "abundance of water" and "numerous wells" are still evident *to this day* (source: en.wikipedia.org/wiki/ Beersheba).

The sacrifice and investment of today produces the joy and abundance of tomorrow. Isaac saw this joy ahead in the promises that God gave to him, and he embraced them by faith and well-digging. He taught his children to be well-diggers and the son from his loins who carried the Blessing continued in his footsteps. The well of Jacob in Samaria, one of many wells that he dug, is also blessing communities *to this day*.

What a legacy! What a testament to the faith of Abraham and Isaac!

Our God is now the God of Abraham, Isaac and Jacob. He is the God of covenant well-diggers. He is the *Lord* of all the lords of the wells that serve Him in Spirit and in truth! Through the exploits and influence of present-day well-diggers, His dominion is extending to the four corners of the Earth!...

Thanks to Isaac and his life of faith!

Join the Isaac Generation!

Heaven is in dire need of a people who will actively assume their God-given roles as kings and priests in the earth. These are people who will not just talk the talk, but will walk their talk through well-digging. No matter the "land" they have been called to possess for God (be it business, politics, media, sports, social spheres, education, entertainment etc.), and no matter the giants that occupy the land, they do not quit digging until they become lords of the wells of their field. Consequently, they influence many in their sphere and become instruments for introducing man to God and God to man. They produce a model people of righteousness, and kings of the earth enquire wisdom from them. They are not shy to testify about the One who is called the Lord of lords of the wells. This is the *Isaac Generation* and you can be a part.

Are you ready to take your position as a lord of the wells in your allotted territory?

How far are you ready to go in establishing the rule of God in your sphere of calling?

What are you doing to prepare for the Gentiles and their kings who will come to the light of your rising?

Are you ready to lay down your life and ambitions for the glory of the Lord of lords and King of kings?

* * *

Welcome! The great company of witnesses in Heaven have been waiting for you to say "yes"!

> *"Arise, shine; for your light has come! And the glory of the Lord is risen upon you. For behold, the darkness shall cover the earth, and deep darkness the people; But the Lord will arise over you, and His glory will be seen upon you. The Gentiles shall come to your light, and kings to the brightness of your rising. Lift up your eyes all around and see: They all gather together, they come to you; your sons shall come from afar, and your daughters shall be nursed at your side. Then you shall see and become radiant, and your heart shall*

*swell with joy; because the abundance of the sea
shall be turned to you, the wealth of the Gentiles
shall come to you.*

*The multitude of camels shall cover your land, the
dromedaries of Median and Ephah; all those from
Sheba shall come; they shall bring gold and
incense, and they shall proclaim the praises
of the Lord.*

*All the flocks of Kedar shall be gathered together
to you, the rams of Nebaioth shall minister to you;
they shall ascend with acceptance on My altar,
and I will glorify the house of My glory."*

(Isaiah 60:1-7)

Join the Well-digger community!

Www.facebook.com/WellDiggerCommunity

GET ALL THE
WELL-DIGGER BOOKS!

The Secret of Abraham

The Wells of Isaac

The Destiny of Jacob

The Greatest Well-Digger in the World

"I am delighted that Tokunbo Emmanuel has developed this thought-provoking series."

- Dr. Hugh Osgood

Other books by
Tokunbo Emmanuel

The Shift of A Lifetime

The Mandate of Paul

Faith Clinic Revival

Run, Church Run!

Ultimate Destiny

The Charismatic Agenda

A Scribe's Inspiration

Rediscovering God

Revival in the Desert

Selah Verses

Sharing the Word of God

The Glory of Young Men

31 Nuggets of Inspiration

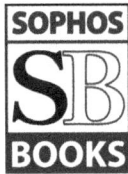

Raising the voice of wisdom!

.

www.ingramcontent.com/pod-product-compliance
Lightning Source LLC
Chambersburg PA
CBHW070539030426
42337CB00016B/2272